Dear Butterfly Heart
"Letters to Chanel"

Dear Butterfly Heart
"Letters to Chanel"

By Barbara K. Lofton

Library of Congress Control Number:		2018914668
ISBN:	Hardcover	978-1-9845-6975-2
	Softcover	978-1-9845-6974-5
	eBook	978-1-9845-6973-8

The views expressed in this work are solely those of the author and do not necessarily reflect the views of the publisher, and the publisher hereby disclaims any responsibility for them.

Scripture quotations marked NIV are taken from the Holy Bible, New International Version®.
NIV®. Copyright © 1973, 1978, 1984 by International Bible Society. Used by permission of Zondervan. All rights reserved. [Biblica]

Scripture quotations marked KJV are from the Holy Bible, King James Version (Authorized Version). First published in 1611. Quoted from the KJV Classic Reference Bible, Copyright ©
1983 by The Zondervan Corporation.

Scripture quotations marked NLT are taken from the Holy Bible, New Living Translation, copyright © 1996, 2004, 2007. Used by permission of Tyndale House Publishers, Inc. Carol Stream, Illinois 60188. All rights reserved. Website.

Any people depicted in stock imagery provided by Getty Images are models, and such images are being used for illustrative purposes only.
Certain stock imagery © Getty Images.

Print information available on the last page.

Rev. date: 01/23/2019

To order additional copies of this book, contact:
Xlibris
1-888-795-4274
www.Xlibris.com
Orders@Xlibris.com
783762

Disclaimer

This book contains thoughts, prayers and poems from Barbara K. Lofton. The material in this book is not to diagnose, treat, cure, or advise on grief or any other health condition. This book is meant to encourage, inspire, and motivate others. People may feel alone, this book is to bring hope and comfort to the reader. Please seek pastoral or professional counseling if you are grieving, depressed, or need help to cope with the death of a loved one or other loss.

This book of poetry is dedicated in the memory of my beautiful daughter, Phillippia Chanel Sanders. She went away without a farewell; she said goodbye to none, but Heaven's gate was wide-open, and a loving voice said, "Come." Our hearts ache, but through the pain, we know she lives on in our memories and through her son. We know that our beloved Chanel is not dead but simply gone. Gone to a better place free of pain and sorrow. A place that we call Heaven. Heaven is where you are resting. You will not come back to us, but one day we will come to you. See you tomorrow. When tomorrow comes, we will rejoice in each other's arms.

Phillippia Chanel Sanders
August 10, 1981–September 6, 2005

"For I know the plans I have for you," declares the Lord, "plans to prosper you and not to harm you, plans to give you hope and a future."
—Jeremiah 29:11 (NIV)

Introduction

The King James Version (KJV) of Jeremiah 29:11 declares, "For I know the thoughts that I think toward you, saith the Lord, thoughts of peace and not of evil to give you an expected end." Do we honestly believe God has plans for us? Do we believe those plans are good and not evil to give us an expected end? If we believe God, then we must take Him at His word. Our faith is certainly tested when a loved one transitions, especially if that loved one is a child. When we lost Chanel, my faith was shaken to the very core. I thought I was doing all the right things by serving God, going to church, praying, living the best way I knew how in the Lord, etc. But still, I lost my child in a tragic car accident. As devastating as that was, I am still here and holding fast to my faith. Do I want to give in at times? Yes! I will never understand why my child had to die. I know I'm not the only parent who has experienced the loss of their child, but it feels as though I am. I'm a parent who feels alone in a world that has forgotten I had a daughter. I feel the weight of never being able to hug my child or spend holidays with her. I will never forget. My survival is praying and trusting God. I often asked myself, "Was I not a good mother?" "Did I do something wrong?" "Did I not love my child enough?" "Was it my fault?" Parents who lose a child (or children) feel a hole in their hearts that can never be filled. There's a void that only God can fill with His love. We may ask, can He? That's where faith pushes out doubt and fear. We should remind ourselves that God is always near. God promised to give us peace that surpasses all understanding. I pray for that peace daily. It's been thirteen years, but it feels like it was only yesterday when I received a call from the morgue telling me to call as soon as possible. I will never forget the feeling that came over me knowing it was Chanel. My Chanel was gone forever. I can't bring her back. Did she want to come back? Couldn't she see the sadness of her son, mother, stepfather, sister, family, and friends? If we certainly believe there is a better place, then we'd think accepting death would be easier. Well, for me it's not. I smile, laugh, and continue to live to adjust my life without my child whom I carried for nine months, connected with in the womb, gave birth to, held for the first time, and kissed her sweet face. I hold on to my memories. My memories keep Chanel alive. I have my family and friends. I have God. I also write. When I think of my baby girl, I cry, but I remember her sweet face and pray for grace. I write how I feel, whether I'm mad, glad, or sad. It's my therapy, my outlet to keep me sane. My heart hurts. It's like a Band-Aid is over the wound, and every birthday, holiday, and special moment when I think of her, the Band-Aid gets pulled back. I have my moments, so I put the Band-Aid back with prayer, prayer, and more prayer. Until I meet my adorable soul again, I will keep living, trusting, and believing her life was not in vain.

I pray, if you, reader, are a parent who lost a child, that this book will be an encouragement for you. I pray this book will bring insight and clarity to you. I pray that you will not feel alone. I pray, when you have a moment of missing your child or a loved one, this book will help you find peace and a little joy to get you through. We all experience loss, whether a death of a loved one, loss of a job, a divorce, an abortion, a miscarriage, loss of a friend or a pet. The loss and the pain are personal. No one can tell you how or how long to grieve. Grief may come and go, but keep going, keep getting help, keep loving yourself, and find comfort through prayer. God loves us, but we must love ourselves first. Loving our self means self-care. Life is filled with topsy-turvy events. Keep your mind on God, and He will keep you in perfect peace.

Peace and love!

God bless and keep you.

Barbara K. Lofton

Prayer of Comfort

".....Death is swallowed up in victory. O death, where is your victory?
O death, where is your sting?"
"For sin is the sting that results in death, and the law
gives sin its power. But thank God! He gives us victory
over sin and death through our Lord Jesus Christ."
—1 Corinthians 15:54b–57 (NLT)

Dear Lord, I pray for all who will read this book inspired by you and my personal loss. I pray they will find joy and serenity in the memories of the person, place, or things they have lost. Lord, You are our provider, our guide, and our strength, in whom we trust. We trust You with our hurt, pain and unknowns. We believe Heaven, one day, will be our gain. Heaven is a place where death will be no more. We will shout and rejoice at last. There will be no need to look back to our past. In the name of Jesus. Amen.

My Heartbeat

My heart is missing a beat. The beat of the one I love.
The beat of my heart is like a song out of rhythm.
Because the one I love is gone.
My heart beats with a skip. The skip in my heart is not a good thing.
My heart beats with a sting.
Because you are not here, how I long for you, my dear.
I yearn for my Heartbeat to be here.
The beat of my heart is out of tune because
my Heartbeat was taken too soon.
The beat of my heart is like a broken record. The
broken pieces I cannot comprehend.
Only God can mend.
My heart is missing a beat, the beat of you, my beloved.
Missing you, my Heartbeat, I really do!

"The LORD is a refuge for the oppressed,
a stronghold in times of trouble."
—Psalm 9:9 NIV

Dear Lord, I felt my daughter's heartbeat, and she felt mine. The beat of our hearts was intertwined. The beat of her heart I can no longer hear. My heart hurts, and I miss her so much. You, Lord, are my refuge and stronghold. When I start missing my heartbeat the most, hold me close, and don't let me go. Wipe away my tears, and give me the fortitude to continue my journey. In the name of Jesus, I pray. Amen.

Reflections:

_____
_____
_____
_____
_____
_____
_____
_____
_____
_____
_____
_____
_____
_____
_____
_____
_____
_____
_____
_____

Favorite Things

Your favorite color was blue. Sometimes blue is
what you felt. Blue was only for a while. God
brought you sunshine to make you smile.
You loved all kinds of animals. You had a dog named Coco
that you loved so. You had a rabbit and you loved Bugs Bunny
too. You loved every living creature. You were going to get
a pet, no matter what Mom said, and that was that.
You loved to swim and fish. Catfish and collard greens
were your favorite dish. You loved having fun and
running in the sun with family and friends.
You loved to read. You had so many books. It seemed like
hundreds at first look. You read novels of romance, mystery,
and comedy. You thought everything was funny.
You loved to dance. Dance was the thing you wanted to do
on stage with your favorite music artist. You would have
accomplished your dream if you were given the chance.
You loved your son. He was your biggest accomplishment.
He brought you joy! Your son was your heart. You
knew he would be from the start. He was one thing you
know you got right. You guys were very tight.
You had so many favorite things, so many dreams, dreams that
were cut short. I pray God's plan is perfect. He knew what He
allowed would be from the day you were born but losing you
was like a thorn. A thorn in our flesh that made us mourn.
He is King of Kings. The omniscient
God, who's grace is sufficient.
He already knew you were "our" favorite thing.

"Every good and perfect gift is from above, coming down from the Father of the heavenly lights, who does not change like shifting shadows."
—James 1:17 NIV

Dear Father, bless all who have experienced loss. As they reminisce about their loved one's favorite places and things, let them rejoice in their memory. Take away the pain, and let them remember their loved one was a gift from You. Thank you for the gift of their life. Help them celebrate the life and legacy their loved one left behind. In Jesus's name. Amen.

Reflections:

_____

_____

_____

_____

_____

_____

_____

_____

_____

_____

_____

_____

_____

_____

_____

_____

_____

_____

_____

_____

_____

Your Son

When you left us, you left a part of you in your son.
He reminds us so much of you. His laugh
and his smile resembles you.
Your son carries your spirit in his eyes. He makes you
alive. I can see your very light shining bright inside.
Your son is like you, so much fun, and his laughter is loud and
proud! It's like God cloned you in the life of your son. He knew
you'd soon be gone, and your precious little one would be our bond.
You left us a beautiful gift, a gift that lifts our spirit
when we are sad. You left us a loving remembrance of
you through your son. For that, we are glad.
Your son is the very replica of your spirit, your
personality, and your strength! God knew what we
needed to fill our empty hearts at length.
Although we have your son, you will be forever missed. God left
us many memories, but your son is number one on the list.

"Children are a heritage from the lord,
offspring a reward from him."
—Psalm 127:3 (NIV)

Dear Lord, thank You for the heritage of children. We bless You for our loved ones who have gone on before us. Our loved ones left their love in the form of their child (children). Their offspring is a reward for us to enjoy. Thank you for the joy and comfort their offspring brings us. Help us to find comfort in loving the ones they left behind. It's the child's spirit that will remind us that our loved is not gone, their spirit lives on in their child. In Jesus's name. Amen.

Reflections:

_____

_____

_____

_____

_____

_____

_____

_____

_____

_____

_____

_____

_____

_____

_____

_____

_____

_____

_____

_____

_____

_____

Why?

I feel the wind; I feel the sunshine rays upon my face;
I hear the birds singing, and I look up to the beautiful
blue sky. Then, I ask the question, "Why?"
Why did you have to leave us at such a very young
age? Why did God allow such great pain to our
hearts? Sometimes it feels like a punishment.
God is an awesome God who created the universe. Couldn't
He have saved you from the terrible accident?
Why does my heart have to hurt? Why couldn't you live to
have more children? Why didn't you fulfill your dreams?
Why did your son have to grow up without his mom?
What is why? Why means for what reason or what
purpose. What was the reason, and what was the purpose
of your death? The Bible says, "All things work together
for the good of them that love God." How will losing
you work out for my good? What was the purpose?
Why does a parent have to bury a child? Why should
a parent have to suffer the what-ifs and the why-mes?
What did I do wrong? Was I not a good parent?
God, in Your infinite wisdom, only You can answer why. I may
not get my answer on this side of glory, but I will trust You,
God, that one day the why will be answered. Help me until Your
glory is revealed. You are the answer, Jesus, the one who heals.
When I take my wings and fly to the sky, when I
see my daughter's face and receive God's ultimate
grace, all the whys will be no more. All the whys I
bore during this race will incredibly be erased.

"And we know that in all things God works for the good of those who love him, who have been called according to his purpose."
—Romans 8:28 (NIV)

Dear Lord, there are so many unanswered questions about death and loss. We often ask, why? Why the loss? Why did our loved one have to die? The pain of loss can be so unbearable. The emptiness we feel when we lose a loved one can bring on so many questions. We trust You to keep us in perfect peace even when the questions go unanswered. Our prayer is that we totally and completely turn our unanswered questions over to You. In Jesus's name. Amen.

Reflections:

_____

_____

_____

_____

_____

_____

_____

_____

_____

_____

_____

_____

_____

_____

_____

_____

_____

_____

_____

_____

_____

_____

_____

I Saw You Today

I saw you today when I pulled back my hair; in me,
I could see your curls and your loving smile.
Your face was visible all the while.
I heard you when I spoke endearment of love to your son.
I heard your laughter echo in my laugh when
I found something that amused me.
I saw you in your son's eyes and his adorable face.
I saw you when I looked out my window and gazed at
the bright sunlight sparkling all over the place.
I remembered your tears when the rain hit my
windshield and was reminded your tears are now
diamonds in your crown of righteousness.
I saw you in the reflection of my face. You are my
seed, an extension of me, and you'll always be.
I miss you, and I wish you were here, but you are here—
in me, your son, your sister, and loved ones. You are not
here physically, but spiritually, you have never left . . .
I thank God you are in a better place. I don't have to fear or
shed another tear because you my dear is evermore here.

He answered, "While the child was still alive, I fasted and wept. I thought, 'Who knows? The lord may be gracious to me and let the child live. But now that he is dead, why should I go on fasting? Can I bring him back again? I will go to him, but he will not return to me."
—*2 Samuel 12:22–23(NIV)*

Lord, thank You for Your amazing grace. Thank You for receiving our loved ones in Your heavenly home. We yearn for them to be here on earth with us. However, we must realize that they will not return to us. Help us see our loved ones in us and the beauty of their memory. Let us celebrate, for one day we will be with them and You. We ask all these things in Jesus's name. Amen.

Reflections:

_____
_____
_____
_____
_____
_____
_____
_____
_____
_____
_____
_____
_____
_____
_____
_____
_____
_____
_____
_____

How to Stop Being Sad

How do we stop being sad when we go through life's storms?
The storms are always tremulous and unsettling. We pray and
seek God for guidance to see us through. No one understands
the trial, not even you. God speaks, but do we listen? His grace
is always there, shining and glistening. How do I stop being
sad? Send praises to God, and He will make me glad!
God is our refuge and strength, a very present help in
trouble. He is our refuge, keeping us safe and sheltering
us from all danger. God soothes our anger.
God is our shield and buckler. He is everything we need. Can we
trust Him? How would it look if my God doesn't come through
for us? Declare I won't be sad! I will rejoice in every situation.
So why do I have fear? God is always near. Why do I feel alone
when God said He would never leave nor forsake me?
Show Yourself, Great and Mighty, like You did when You
parted the Red Sea! Show Yourself, Great and Mighty, like
You did when Jesus rose from the dead after three days in
the tomb. Give me assurance You're coming soon. Stop being
sad and full of gloom. It is destined to be your doom.
I need You to lift the spirt of heaviness from me. You said, for
the spirit of heaviness, put on the garment of praise. Help me
worship You because worship brings me into Your presence
and gladness! Worship brings me into Your anointing. It's
Your anointing that destroys the yoke of sadness! Your spirt
brings gladness. This is how I stop being sad; pray and ask
God to break every chain and destroy every yoke! Praise
Him for your breakthrough, the Father adores you!

"And it shall come to pass in that day, that his burden shall be taken away from off thy shoulder, and his yoke from off thy neck, and the yoke shall be destroyed because of the anointing."
—Isaiah 10:27 (KJV)

Dear Lord, losing a loved one can be burdensome and can cause great sadness. We want to live in happiness, not guilt. You are our keeper. Keep us in a place of gladness in spite of our life tests and trials. Father, destroy the yoke of sadness, depression, guilt, anger, and denial. Anoint us with Your grace and peace. Continue to cover us in Your love and free us of grief. In Jesus's name. Amen.

Reflections:

_____

_____

_____

_____

_____

_____

_____

_____

_____

_____

_____

_____

_____

_____

_____

_____

_____

_____

_____

Tired

I am tired of being alone. I'm tired of phony people. Yes, in life,
we all have our ups and downs, but when will people stop being
selfish and encourage someone who is always encouraging them?
I am tired of the imitators and all the haters. I try to
remember they are just my motivators and the elevator that
is taking me to a new level toward my divine destiny.
Stop pretending to be someone or something you are not
because I'm tired of your imitating and hating. Why can't you
congratulate and motivate, instead of always wanting to hate?
God created a bouquet of flowers; none have the same design
or color or pattern. So why do you try to pattern your life like
mine? God didn't create a boring, bland universe. He created
a magnificent masterpiece when He created the earth. God
knew something was missing, so He created each person
in His image; unique and wonderful. Don't curse your life
trying to be a double when all it does is cause you trouble.
I am tired of empty promises and people who tell lies. Have integrity!
Your word flies with a lot of weight. Learn to congratulate not hate!
I am tired of the empty nest that came to soon. It's such a gloom.
We give birth to our babies and raised them up. We can't wait until
they are grown to get go out on their own. We have to cherish every
moment. It's not easy being alone. I am tired of the silence that was
pushed upon me way to soon. No more laughter, no more arguing,
and no more yelling, just a quiet empty place in my heart and in
my space. I am tired of feeling alone. God, where is Your grace?
The Bible tells us to be not weary in well doing,
for we shall reap if we faint not.
So don't be tired of who you are. Don't stop encouraging
and exhorting the people who don't return the same

to you. God knows, and He is watching. He sees your
heart. Tomorrow is a new start with new mercies.
So take your tired spirit and lay it before the King because
He declares He will be with us through everything.

"Let us not become weary in doing good, for at the proper time we will reap a harvest if we do not give up."
—Galatians 6:9 (NIV)

Dear Lord, We ask for Your Holy Spirit to strengthen us mind, body and soul. We have experienced hurt, loss, pain, and so many tears. Your word tells us not to get tired of always doing what is right. We should always do good. We should treat people right and live in Your loving light. We believe that at the right time, You will reward our good deeds. We will reap a harvest of joy, peace, grace, healing and all You have for us. In Jesus's name. Amen.

Reflections:

_____

_____

_____

_____

_____

_____

_____

_____

_____

_____

_____

_____

_____

_____

_____

_____

_____

_____

_____

_____

Sometimes

Sometime I feel sad; sometimes I feel glad. I feel sad because there is a piece of my heart that was taken away. Sometimes I feel sad because I'm glad. I don't want you to think I am glad and have forgotten you are not with me anymore. Sometimes when I am glad, I feel guilt. Guilt of being glad. I even get mad. Why did I lose my child? Why can't I see her beautiful face and lovely smile? Why do I have to feel sad when I want to feel glad? God, give me gladness to fill the sadness. How can I continue my life with a smile but behind the smile is sadness? Sadness in my heart that you baby girl is no longer a part of my life on earth? I pray, and I press. I cry, and I smile in my sadness knowing that even though I'm sad, you are glad, glad to be in heaven with the Lord, watching and waiting for me to be glad because you are glad. But still, sometimes I feel sad . . . Sometimes I cry. I can't control the tears. They come at unexpected times. Just when I think, "I'm going to be okay this time," tears and fears fill my heart. Then I'm back to the start, the start of why my child? Why these tears and unsure years, years without your hugs and smiles? A life on earth without you, sometimes I think this can't be true. Sometimes I just sit and watch for a sign, a sign of time that you are fine. Sometimes I feel mad but mostly, I feel glad. I'm glad God has you in the palm of His hand. So I remind myself not to be sad. Sometimes . . .

Sorrow is better than laughter, for sadness
has a refining influence on us.
—Ecclesiastes 7:3 (NLT)

Dear Lord, I don't want to be sad. I want to be joyful. How can I experience joy when there is so much pain? Send Your peace, and fill me with Your joy. Your joy is everlasting. Your word declares in our sorrow that You refine us. You make us better. We don't always understand how, but we trust You that our sadness will be refined pure as gold. In the name of Jesus. Amen.

Reflections:

_____

_____

_____

_____

_____

_____

_____

_____

_____

_____

_____

_____

_____

_____

_____

_____

_____

_____

_____

_____

Void

There is a void in my heart. A void of emptiness, hurt, and pain. A void that tears my soul apart. A void in my heart that no one can understand. A void of not knowing that you are okay. A void that I can't explain. A void of not seeing you grow older or live out your life with your son. A void of not seeing your sister graduate from law school. A void that makes me feel like a fool. A void of feeling completely empty. A void that God said He can fill, He can fill with joy and peace. A void that only God can cure. A void that will someday no more to endure.

"I pray that God, the source of hope, will fill you completely with joy and peace because you trust in him. Then you will overflow with confident hope through the power of the Holy Spirit."
—Romans 15:13 (NLT)

Dear Lord, take away the void. Fill me completely with Your unspeakable joy and overflowing peace. I trust You. My hope is in You. Fill this void with Your Holy Spirit that empowers me with hope and confidence. In Jesus's name. Amen.

Reflections:

_____

_____

_____

_____

_____

_____

_____

_____

_____

_____

_____

_____

_____

_____

_____

_____

_____

_____

_____

_____

_____

_____

_____

Trade It All

People see you with your house, your car, your
clothes, and your style. They don't know that all the
while, you would trade it all for your child.
The material things are nothing; they will perish. It's
you that I cherish. I would trade it all just to have
you back with me; that's how I want it to be.
The material things are not my life; life is all because
of Christ! That is how I strive and survive.
People look at my confidence and think I have it all together, but
they don't know I would trade it all just for one more phone call.
They don't know my story or the reason for God's glory. They
judge my praise and shout without knowing what it is all about.
I would trade a lifetime of things just to have your very being.
I would trade it all if you could be here. I
would trade it all for you to be near.
I would trade it all regardless of the fall; I would trade it all.

*"Wherever your treasure is, there the desires
of your heart will be also be."*
—Matthew 6:21 (NLT)

Heavenly Father, we love You first because You first loved us. We love our family and friends so dearly. Help us to never put You or those we love before You. You are the one and true God; the God who helps us through all trials and difficulties in life, the God who saved us with Your amazing grace. Grace is the greatest gift which by we are saved. All that we have materially is because of You. Our material possessions are nothing without You and those we love. In the matchless name of Jesus I pray. Amen.

Reflections:

_____
_____
_____
_____
_____
_____
_____
_____
_____
_____
_____
_____
_____
_____
_____
_____
_____
_____
_____
_____

Blessed

When you were born, I was very proud. I was so excited! I felt like
I was floating on a cloud. I realized this little life in my hands was
a gift from God. And all I wanted was for her to be blessed.
As you begin to grow and started to walk then talk, reality
set in—you wouldn't be a baby long. Your personality was
very strong. You held your own. I prayed for God to cover
you and give you a life filled with blessings and not strife.
When you became teenager, I sometimes worried that life would go
by in a hurry. So I strived to be the best mother. Your life was like
no other. God did have you covered, covered with blessings of favor
and grace, favor and grace to grow into your own to run your race.
As you grew into a young woman, you had to deal with
some struggles. The struggles were hard. But the struggles
could not stop the hand of God's plan for your life. The
struggles were just a weapon that could not prosper.
They couldn't prosper because you were blessed.
All I ever wanted was for you to be blessed, blessed
with a life filled with hope and dreams, a life filled
with love cascading like streams into a river.
I prayed that you would always be blessed, blessed
with God's very best. Now I know you are blessed.
You're living your blessed life now in Heaven.

"The LORD bless you and keep you; the LORD make his face shine on you and be gracious to you; the LORD turn his face toward you and give you peace."
—Numbers 6:24–25

Heavenly Father, bless us with Your favor to stay strong until we see our loved ones again. Shine Your peace upon our hearts. We need Your omnipotent power to sustain us. Let us keep our eyes on You and not on grief, sufferings, and pain. You are Jehovah Rapha, the God who heals. Heal our wounds and wipe away every tear and all fear. Bless and keep us until we meet again. In Jesus's name. Amen.

Reflections:

_____

_____

_____

_____

_____

_____

_____

_____

_____

_____

_____

_____

_____

_____

_____

_____

_____

_____

_____

_____

Butterfly Heart

I am a mother who grieves for my child. You say its
fine; give it time. Grief may take a while.
How long is a while? A second, a minute, a day, an hour,
a year? How do you know? Have you seen my tears? Have
you felt my fear? I lost my baby who was so dear.
Who is to say how one should grieve or how
long this horrible pain should be?
I am a mother who lost part of her heart. Why should I be told when,
how, and where to start? What is it to grieve? When will it leave?
I just want my butterfly heart, my baby, my child, the
one who was formed in my womb, changing and growing
into a living, breathing, and beautiful being.
I am a mother who will always miss her child. God, help me
through the pain, the grief, and the missing piece of my life.
My heart will forever grieve, miss, and long for my child
until Heaven is my home. In Heaven my butterfly and
I will be together at last. Alas! In Heaven, no more of
what has been. In Heaven my heart will mend.

"He heals the brokenhearted and bandages their wounds."
Psalm 147:3 (NLT)

Heavenly Father, as we come to you with our cares and concerns. Help us to totally surrender all to You. We are weak and wounded. You, Lord, are our healer. You hold us in Your loving arms. We may not understand our loss, but we know You are faithful to get us through all circumstances. You promised in your word to heal the brokenhearted and bandage our wounds. It's not easy, but we trust in Your sovereignty. Continue to care for us. Cover us. Lift us when we are in despair. In the precious name of Jesus. Amen.

Reflections:

_____
_____
_____
_____
_____
_____
_____
_____
_____
_____
_____
_____
_____
_____
_____
_____
_____
_____
_____
_____

I Love My Life

I love my life.
I may have ups and downs,
I have shed some tears,
and I have some fears,
but I love my life.
I may have lost loved ones and friends
or paid the cost
but I love my life.
God has been good.
He said He would.
He has never failed.
I may frown,
I may clown,
I hurt,
and I love.
I thank God, the man above,
for my life.
My life is good;
my life is blessed.
It's not always the best.
I have stood some tests.
I fall short,
but God knows my heart.
I love my life.
My life is a journey,
a journey that many cannot handle.
They may think they can but they can't hold a candle.
I look back, and I can actually say
I love my life.
Step back devil, you have no victory over my life!
My life is blessed. In spite of the test!

"Be thankful in all circumstances, for this is God's
will for you who belong to Christ Jesus."
—1 Thessalonians 5:18 (NLT)

Dear Lord, You said to be thankful in all we go through in this life.
How can we be thankful when we have lost someone so dear to our
hearts? Life can be so hard. You, God, feel our pain. You sent Your
only Son to die. Jesus, healed all our pain and sorrow when he died on
the cross. He gave us hope for tomorrow. As we observe life, help us to
count our many blessings and be thankful. It may not be the life we've
planned. However, Your plans for our life will always stand. Let us be
thankful in all circumstances knowing You are in control. In Jesus's
name. Amen.

Reflections:

_____

_____

_____

_____

_____

_____

_____

_____

_____

_____

_____

_____

_____

_____

_____

_____

_____

_____

When I Get There

Chile, when I get there, we will dance, sing, and shout. We will
dance about. I miss you, but I know you wouldn't trade Heaven
for a return ticket to days like these. These days are filled with
hatred, murder, disaster, sickness, and disease. You are at peace
and resting, waiting for me. You are home with the Master.
When I get there, what a day of rejoicing! All my questions
will be answered. When I get there, I won't be sad but glad.
When I get there, I will be forever full of laughter.
When I get there, I wanna see your face. We will be in a happy
place. When I get there, all the time we lost will be rekindled!
The time that dwindled will no longer be remembered!
We will be jolly, happy and full in our hearts! I will hug
and love on you. All I prayed about will reign true!
When I get there, I won't feel low. Cause I will see
you and Jesus aglow! Oh, the love Jesus will bestow! A
love to heal our hearts. His blessings to impart! All the
heartache I felt from losing you will quickly depart!
As I continue to live my life down here, my goal is for my
soul to make it there. Save a seat for me my dear. I will walk
through the pearly gates having no fear. My arrival will
be right on time! Our God is never late and He make no
mistakes. Until I get there to the place we call "Heaven",
I will keep believing and trusting God with my all.
When I get there, I will know the times I was
crying for you, you were crying for me.
Crying and cheering me on to get there too.
When I get there, I will no longer be blue. I will
be so elated to see the new glorious you!

"But we are citizens of heaven, where the Lord Jesus Christ lives. And we are eagerly waiting for him to return as our Savior. He will take our weak mortal bodies and change them into glorious bodies like his own, using the same power with which he will bring everything under his control."

—Philippians 3:20-21 (NLT)

Dear Lord, we eagerly await Your arrival. Give us confidence that we will see our loved ones again in Heaven. Your word says our bodies are not our home. We will have new glorious bodies like Yours! You have a home for us with You to live forever. Help us not to focus on this life but by faith keep striving for our heavenly home with You. In the name of Jesus. Amen.

Reflections:

_____

_____

_____

_____

_____

_____

_____

_____

_____

_____

_____

_____

_____

_____

_____

_____

_____

_____

_____

A Heart of Gold

Yours was a heart of gold. You are a beautiful soul. You
are missed beyond measure, but you are now God's
treasure. We were created for His pleasure.
He called you home where we all belong. It was
your time to go, but it still hurts so.
You were a joy to be around. You always acted a clown. You lifted
those who were down. No need to frown when you were around.
You always gave your last even if it meant you wouldn't have.
You had a heart of gold. Your story will never
go untold. You are a beautiful soul.
We will always miss your bold, beautiful life. Until we
meet again, your heart of gold will be like a stole covering
our hearts and minds until the end of time.

"As a face is reflected in water, so the
heart reflects the real person."
—Proverbs 27:19 (NLT)

Dear Lord, let our memories of our loved one ease the hurt we feel of not having them here with us. Help us remember their laughter, joy, and love they gave us. Their memory is our peace and comfort when we miss them most. Let us cherish the heart of gold they possessed. Having them for the time we did makes us blessed. In Jesus's name. Amen.

Reflections:

_____

_____

_____

_____

_____

_____

_____

_____

_____

_____

_____

_____

_____

_____

_____

_____

_____

_____

_____

_____

_____

_____

_____

_____

The Butterfly Visit

A butterfly came to visit me today. I was so amazed
because of the long stay. I took pictures and videotaped.
This butterfly came to let me know your spirit still lives
on in every way, even though you could not stay.
The butterfly visit was so sweet. I spoke to her with gentleness and
ever so meek because I knew she was my sign in the presence of time.
The butterfly visit was divine, a heavenly encounter to
ponder. I felt your spirit, there was no need to wonder.
I couldn't believe she was dressed in your favorite color
of blue, which definitely meant it was a sign from you.
I thank God for the butterfly visit. God cares for us left
behind. He wants us to know our loved ones are fine.
The butterfly visit made me shed a few tears. Deep in my
heart, I knew you were near. I miss you so much. The butterfly
visit was so dear. I whispered I love you, but I did not fear.
The butterfly visit was clear. You, my love, will always be
here. Thank you, God, for my butterfly visit. It gave me
absolute peace, a reassurance Chanel will always be near.

"And the peace of God, which transcends all understanding,
will guard your hearts and your minds in Christ Jesus."
— Philippians 4:7 (NIV)

Dear Lord, I give You glory and praise for every sign You have given me that my loved one's spirit lives on. Thank You for the peace that only You can give peace that no one can understand. Your peace keeps us in all life storms. Thank You for guarding our hearts and mind. In Jesus's name. Amen.

Reflections:

_____
_____
_____
_____
_____
_____
_____
_____
_____
_____
_____
_____
_____
_____
_____
_____
_____
_____
_____
_____
_____
_____

I'm Free

Like butterflies on a cool, summer, morning breeze, I'm
free. Don't worry about me. See I am free—free from the
pain and suffering of the world. I'm free as I can be.
Like the dragonflies, my wings are spread, no need to dread.
I'm not dead but a free spirit. My soul is resting on.
Like the birds in the air, you have no need to
worry. I know it's scary, but I'm free.
When you feel the cool breeze or the warm sunshine on
your face, keep in mind, I'm free. No more death, sickness,
sadness, depression or loneliness. I'm flying free. My
wings are spread; Heaven is my home. Don't feel alone.
I'm always by your side. I will be your forever guide.
Butterflies, dragonflies, and me, flying free. No
chains holding me. I'm free, I'm free, I am free!
Don't you dare cry or sigh. I am flying high!
I'm free. Isn't this what you wanted for me?

"So if the Son sets you free, you are truly free."
—John 8:36 (NLT)

Dear Heavenly Father, thank You for setting us free, free from sin and death. Our loved one is truly free when they are home in Heaven with You. One day we to pray for the ultimate freedom in Your Kingdom. Let us not weep but rejoice that they are free! Thank You, Lord, they have the uttermost freedom. We pray in Jesus's name. Amen.

Reflections:

_____

_____

_____

_____

_____

_____

_____

_____

_____

_____

_____

_____

_____

_____

_____

_____

_____

_____

_____

_____

_____

_____

_____

Hope

I have hope to see you again. Again, in Heaven, we both win!
Hope to know you are happy and safe. Living in an amazing place!
Hope that my fears and tears will be erased.
Hope for God's surpassing peace. Peace no one can understand.
Hope of light in the darkest of days.
Hope of joy when I am sad. The joy of
your memories to make me glad.
Hope that God only chooses the best. The
best to watch over us in our mess.
Hope of anticipation is mine. Anticipating
when I see you one more time.

*"And now, dear brothers and sisters, we want you to
know what will happen to the believers who have died
so you will not grieve like people who have no hope. For
since we believe that Jesus died and was raised to life
again, we also believe that when Jesus returns, God will
bring back with him the believers who have died."*
—*1 Thessalonians 4:13–14 NLT*

Dear Lord, it's hard to remain in hope and faith when a portion of your heart is taken away. Each day should be better, but my hope sometimes waver. Give me the power of Your Holy Spirit to continue in hope that Jesus died that we may live. Hope to know with assurance I will see Your glory and my loved one again. In Jesus's name. Amen.

Reflections:

_____

_____

_____

_____

_____

_____

_____

_____

_____

_____

_____

_____

_____

_____

_____

_____

_____

_____

Release

Release me, and let me go. I can't stay with you here on earth anymore. I will always be by your side. I can see Heaven's door. Release me now so I can abide in the heavenly realm, the heavenly realm to be with God whom I adore.
Release me, and let me be free. I hear God's voice calling me. I wish I could stay, but letting me go is the key, key to my eternal gain and your sweet refrain.
Release me, and let my spirit flow to Heaven. Heaven is my home now. There is no need for you to be weary. There is no need for you to cry. Keep your eyes to the sky. I'm your angel wrapped in love, watching over you continuously from above. Release me so I can achieve what God intended for me. Earth is not our home. I'm only gone, gone to a place where we will meet again, a place free of harm and sin. Don't fret or worry.
Don't try to hold me in a place that is not my space. Release me, and let me go. Stand in faith, be bold, and cherish my soul. My soul is at rest. There's no need to guess. God knows best. Release me, and let me go. I will be with you in spirit, always and forevermore.

For we know that if the earthly tent we live in is destroyed, we have a building from God, an eternal house in heaven, not built by human hands.
—2 Corinthians 5:1

Dear Lord, we have to be honest in our prayers to You and admit it's hard to let go of our loved ones. We do not understand death but pray in faith that one day we will meet our loved ones again. Help us release our loved one to You. Show us how to continue to live without them physically and believe that their spirit will forever be by our side. In the precious name of Jesus. Amen.

Reflections:

_____

_____

_____

_____

_____

_____

_____

_____

_____

_____

_____

_____

_____

_____

_____

_____

_____

_____

_____

_____

Get Up!

Get up; life is waiting on you. You have a lot of living to do!
Get up; keep your loved one's memory alive. Alive
so you can live on until you meet again.
Get up; move toward your destiny. You are still here for a
purpose and a plan. God has you in the palm of His hand.
Get up; move forward. Don't get lost in
grief. Grief is stopping your life.
Get up! Stop putting your very being on hold. Go forth and be
bold. It's time to shine! Shine for the love you loss. Go be a boss!
Get up; time is wasting.
Get up; don't you dare just lay there!
Get up, and put on your Sunday best. In spite of it all, you are blessed!
Get up; it's a new day! Get up, you are alive! It's not your time!
Get up, you have some living to do. Don't feel guilty or
sad when you start to live. Living is the most you can
give to those you love and to the ones gone on.
Get up, life is waiting on you!
Get up and live! Live in the now! Live the best you know how!

"No test or temptation that comes your way is beyond the course of what others have had to face. All you need to remember is that God will never let you down; he'll never let you be pushed past your limit; he'll always be there to help you come through it."
—1 Corinthians 10:13 MSG

Dear Lord, You are our merciful Father. You are Lord of Lord and King of Kings! You are mighty and great! You are able to keep us through any hardship. Please bless the ones who are encumbered with grief. They are weary and worn out from the pain of loss. Help them move forward without guilt, shame or doubt. God, You said in Your word that You would be our comforter, our guide and our way out! Strengthen those who are left behind to continue to live here on earth without those they love. Remind them that there is hope, and You won't put more on us than we can bear. We declare and decree it to be so! In the name of Jesus our wonderful Savior. Amen.

Reflections:

_____

_____

_____

_____

_____

_____

_____

_____

_____

_____

_____

_____

_____

_____

_____

_____

_____

Conclusion

"For I can do everything through Christ, who gives me strength."
—Philippians 4:13 NLT

"He gives power to the weak and strength to the powerless."
Isaiah 40:29 NLT

I pray that this book has been a blessing to you and will continue to give you hope has you use it for your daily devotional. I must admit, even though I have a big part of my heart missing, I do have a blessed life. God continues to give me grace and more grace. He moves me from faith to faith. I would love for my daughter to be here with us enjoying this life. If I believe the word of God, her life is better now. Her life down here was over at twenty-four years old. This fact is hard to accept. Life for me has been rearranged and readjusted since my daughter transitioned. I have to keep moving forward in faith and prayer that one day I will see Chanel again. I have faith that she is happy and living in Heaven with Jesus. My faith is what keeps me grounded. My faith is what pushes me out of the bed each day. My faith is what keeps me from screaming at the top of my lungs, *why?* Faith is my foundation, being rooted and grounded in Jesus which keeps me from losing my mind. My faith started a long time ago as a child, but life situations has caused me to draw closer to the throne room. My faith and prayer give me hope. We have to believe what the Bible says. In Christ, we have victory in all things! Even in death! Death has no victory over us! We have to remain in faith from day to day if we want a future. Being stuck in pain and sorrow can't move us to the destiny that God has for us. Believe that your loved one's life was not in vain; be thankful for the years you spent with them. Set your mind on things above, and let God lead you along the way. Grow from faith to faith each day. Tell yourself that you're going to make it. Speak life and you shall live! There is power in what we speak! Yes, you will have some sad days and good days, but keep moving in faith. Make your loved one proud. Let their memory be spoken out loud. Get up and do something! Don't waste another day. Life is short! You have a destiny to fulfill. The Bible declares in Romans, "And we know that all things work together for good to them that love God, to them who are the called according to his purpose." Have faith in knowing it will work out for your good.

For His Glory!

Keep the faith! Holding on to His grace!

Shalom!

Barbara K. Lofton

I wish Heaven had a phone, so I could hear your voice again. I thought of you today, but that's nothing new. I thought about you yesterday and days before that too. I think of you in silence. I often speak your name. All I have are memories and a picture in a frame.
—Unknown

We Remembered

Written on January 6, 2015

It's been ten years—ten years I have lived and survived without you by my side. How did I make it without you? I remember the day you left. I thought I would never be able to walk, talk, eat sing, dance, survive or thrive! It's been ten years of no laughter, no smile, and no hugs, none of your love. I still don't understand why, and I still cry. Why? For ten years, your son has been without his mom, your sister has not seen her big sister, and your Ronnie has not been able to mow the lawn or have fun with you. For ten years, your family and friends have missed, longed for, cried, and wondered why you had to leave us at such an early age. God gave you to us on loan for twenty-four years. It seems so unfair. Twenty-four years don't seem long at all, but we all must recall that the Bible declares that our life is just a vapor. It's here, and then it's gone. To me, it feels so wrong. Oh, how I long for you, I cry for you, I pray for you, and still, I have to go on. I have to keep pressing, pushing, and praying. I have to be strong and trust that God didn't allow no wrong. His purpose is strong. His plans are sure. God has kept me for ten years. Please, Lord, keep my mind, my heart, my soul, and my existence until we meet again. I still can't believe I have lived, strived, and survived without you for ten years. If it had not been for my faith, my fate would have been worse. My life would be cursed. Thank God for His strength and His grace that keeps us from day to day. You were twenty-four when you died on the sixth day of September, two plus four equals six. So yesterday we paid tributes to you, Chanel! The place you were born and baptized (at age eleven) was at Fort Campbell, Kentucky; the place you transitioned was at Evans, Georgia; and your resting place, Altus, Oklahoma, and Chicago! We cherish your memories always.

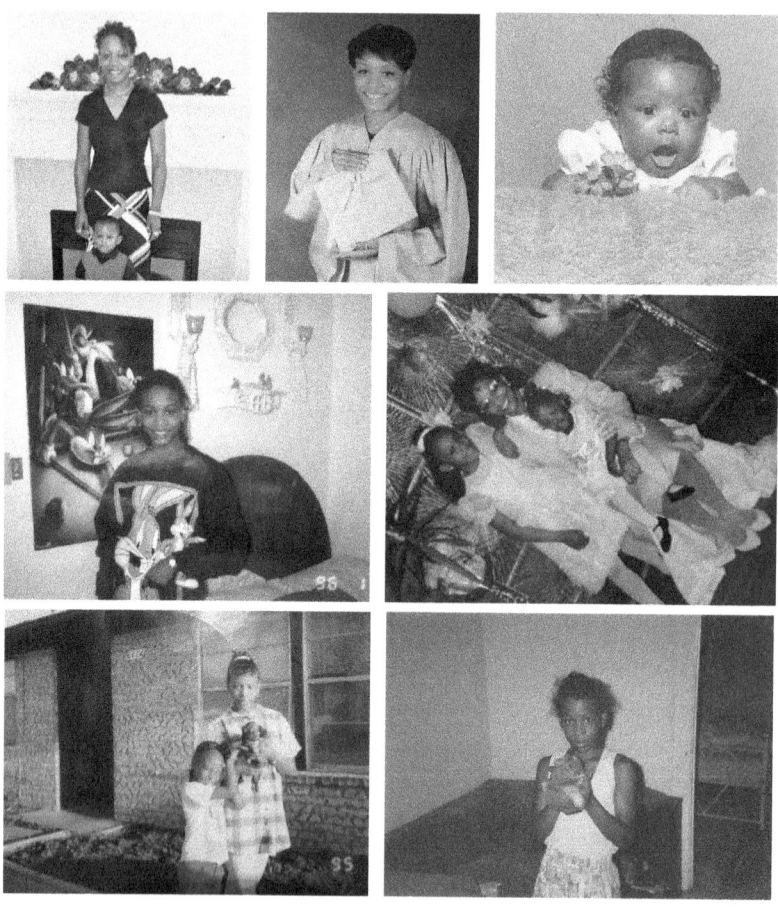

In Remembrance
of
Phillippia Chanel Sanders

Dear Father,
Thank You for the life and legacy of Phillippia Chanel Sanders.
Thank You for the joyfulness she brought to us all. Thank You for
gifting us with her presence for twenty-four years. We remember her
today and always with joy and happiness that only You can give. We
miss her so much, but her spirit lives on with You and in our hearts.
We love and trust You, God, so we know we shall meet again. Keep
us in perfect peace. In the quiet times, speak to us and touch our
minds to rejoice knowing that Chanel's life did not end on September
6, 2005; it was only the beginning. In Jesus's name. Amen!

Scriptures of Comfort for Grief

He will wipe every tear from their eyes. There will
be no more death or mourning or crying or pain,
for the old order of things has passed away.
—Revelation 21:4 (NIV)

The Lord is close to the brokenhearted and
saves those who are crushed in spirit.
—Psalm 34:18 (NIV)

Give all your worries and cares to God, for He cares for you.
—1 Peter 5:7 (NLT)

Now when Jesus saw the crowds, he went up on a
mountainside and sat down. His disciples came to him,
and he began to teach them. He said, "Blessed are the
poor in spirit, for theirs is the kingdom of heaven."
—Matthew 5:1–3 (NIV)

My flesh and my heart may fail, but God is the
strength of my heart and my portion forever.
—Psalm 73:26 (NIV)

Do not let your hearts be troubled. You
believe in God; believe also in me.
—John 14:1 (NIV)

Have I not commanded you? Be strong and courageous.
Do not be afraid; do not be discouraged, for the Lord
your God will be with you wherever you go.
—Joshua 1:9 (NIV)

The Lord gives strength to his people; the
Lord blesses his people with peace.
—Psalm 29:11 (NIV)

Blessed are those who mourn, for they will be comforted.
—Matthew 5:4 (NIV)

Scriptures for Encouragement

The LORD is close to all who call on him, yes,
to all who call on him in truth.
He grants the desires of those who fear him; he
hears their cries for help and rescues them.
—Psalms 145:18–19 (NLT)

Ask me and I will tell you remarkable secrets
you do not know about things to come.
—Jeremiah 33:3 (NLT)

Give your burdens to the LORD, and he will take care of
you. He will not permit the godly to slip and fall.
—Psalms 55:22 (NLT)

Don't be afraid, for I am with you. Don't be discouraged,
for I am your God. I will strengthen you and help you.
I will hold you up with my victorious right hand.
—Isaiah 41:10 (NLT)

Trust in the LORD with all your heart; do not depend
on your own understanding. Seek his will in all you
do, and he will show you which path to take.
—Proverbs 3:5–6 (NLT)

When you pass through the waters, I will be with you;
and when you pass through the rivers, they will sweep
over you. When you walk through the fire, you will
not be burned; the flames will not set you ablaze.
—Isaiah 43:2 (NIV)

To all who mourn in Israel, he will give a crown of beauty for
ashes, a joyous blessing instead of mourning, festive praise
instead of despair. In their righteousness, they will be like
great oaks that the LORD has planted for his own glory.
—Isaiah 61:3 (NLT)

Grief

Grief: deep sorrow, especially that caused by someone's death.

My definition of grief is a loss that can never be physically returned. It's an emotional roller coaster that will twist and turn you upside down at the least unexpected moment.

What does grief mean to you?

_____
_____
_____
_____
_____
_____
_____
_____
_____
_____
_____
_____
_____
_____
_____
_____

Hope

Hope: a feeling of expectation and desire for a certain thing to happen.

My definition of hope: Healing, Optimism, and Purpose are Expectation because of God!

Healing from hurt and pain. Optimistic about the outcome of the loss of my loved one. There is a purpose for the transition. I'm expecting all these things to come to pass because of God!

What is your definition of hope?

_____

_____

_____

_____

_____

_____

_____

_____

_____

_____

_____

_____

_____

_____

Acknowledgments

I would like to thank God for giving me the courage and strength to write this book. I thank God for giving us strength to live without Chanel. Without Him, we can't do anything.

To my loving husband Ronnie for always, always, supporting me in all my endeavors. I love you very much, and I am grateful for your unconditional love and support.

I want to thank my mother, Sherry West Dykes, for my Christian upbringing. I would not be the woman I am today if not for your love for God, me, and others. I am inspired to be just like you.

To my daughter Jasmine, I am so proud of you. Keep doing what you're doing. Your hard work will pay off soon! Always strive to do your best. I love you more than you know.

To my grandson Marquise, life without you would be unbearable. I thank God that your Mom left us the gift of you. Your love is what I need to continue to move forward. Marquise, we are proud of you, and we are sure your Mom is too.

To my entire family, you are the best! Family means everything to me. I love you all. Thanks for being in my corner and praying without ceasing for us.

Thanks to my ride or die friends (you know who you are) who have been with me through it all! Your motivation and prayers enable me to remain strong in spite of everything. Thanks for being with me on this journey. I love you, forever friends.

To all parents who have experienced the tremendous loss of a child, I salute you. Keep moving forward. Keep praying. Keep your faith. Keep smiling. Keep your child's memory alive. Remember, you are not alone. God has us covered. Continued prayers for you. I hold you in my heart.

To everyone who has ever whispered a word of prayer or said an encouraging word to me, thank you. Your earnest concern for me means a lot. Again, thanks everyone!

The Grave

Lord help me to remember Chanel is not here,
Her body was laid in the grave, but she now
has a marvelous life that you gave.
The grave is a holding place for the dust and ashes from
which she came. Her spirit lives on the same.
The grave is a place to visit and to remember she lived. Not
forgetting that she was here and so deeply revered. The grave
could not hold her in this space because You, Dear God,
were waiting there to transition her soul in the air.

References

Merriam-Webster's Dictionary online

New Living Translation (NLT), New International Version (NIV), King James Version (KJV), and The Message (MSG) from Bible.com and YouVersion.com app copyright 1973, 1984, 2001 by Bibles, Inc. Used by permission.

Biblegateway.com

Author Contact Information:

Contact info:

https://barbaralofton.com/home/

www.barbaraloftonministries.com

www.facebook.com   - Barbara K. Lofton; The Cost of Favor

@barbara_lofton7 on Instagram.

CPSIA information can be obtained
at www.ICGtesting.com
Printed in the USA
BVHW031121150519
548352BV00007B/70/P

9 781984 569752